The PRINCESS and the PEAS

Abby Jackson

Illustrated by Tammy Smith

Rigby®

A Harcourt Achieve Imprint

www.Rigby.com
1-800-531-5015

Once there was a princess
who was smart and very kind.
Behind her castle, she kept
a beautiful garden.
She loved this garden
more than anything.

The princess grew yellow corn,
carrots, and sweet green peas.
The peas were hard to take care of,
but she loved them.
She took extra good care of them.

Each day, the princess worked
in her garden.
Sometimes, however, she was lonely.
The princess wanted to share
her garden with a prince.

Many young men came to see
the princess.
Not one of them was a real prince.

What was the sign of a real prince?
The princess thought about it,
and wrote a poem.

A real prince
Will always know,
How to make
The green peas grow.

The next morning, another
young man came by.
"Will you help me pull weeds?"
she asked him.

He was happy to help the princess.

The prince began to pull weeds.
"You don't need these ugly vines,"
he said.

"No, No! Stop!" cried the princess.
"Don't pull those.
They are my green peas!"

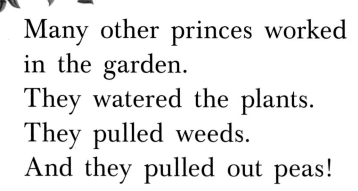

Many other princes worked
in the garden.
They watered the plants.
They pulled weeds.
And they pulled out peas!

Soon there was only one small vine of peas left.

The princess was very sad. "I doubt that I will ever find my real prince," she said.

The next day, another young man
walked by.
He didn't look like the princes.
His clothes were not fancy,
and he looked tired and hungry.

The princess asked him to work
in the garden.

The young man worked hard
in the garden.
He pulled weeds and made sure
the plants had no bugs.
He saw the one small vine,
and he knew it was not a weed.
He took good care of it.

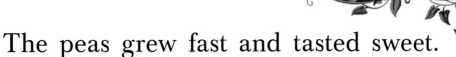

The peas grew fast and tasted sweet.

One day, the princess and the young man picked some of the peas.

"These are better than any peas I've ever eaten!" said the princess.

The princess knew she had found her real prince at last.

She asked, "Will you peas . . . I mean *please* be my prince?"

The two of them lived happily ever after.